A Children's Book of Poems

Book III

Ernest Bevin Academy

Contents

Title Page

Copyright

Inspirational Quotes

Introduction

I Wonder by Inam Ali	1
A Perfect World by Niraj Kuganathan	2
Each Other by Connor Langley	4
A Perfect World by Zaheer Gani	5
Peace Not War by Abdullah Hoque	6
A Perfect World by Robin Concepcion	7
A Perfect World by Malick Dieng Diallo	8
A Perfect World by Oskar Maciag	9
A Perfect World by Ryad Muir	10
A Perfect World by Robin Concepcion	11
Through the Eyes of the Earth by Rory Langan	13
Through their Eyes is Beauty by Jon-Lewis Odhiambo	15

A Perfect World by Sedad Assen	17
Freedom by Jack Broome	18
Freedom by Robin Concepcion	19
Freedom by Malick Dieng Diallo	20
Freedom by Freddy Sheedy	21
Love is in the Air by Jibril Abdul Wahab	23
An Unreachable World by Asvinth Sooriyapalan	24
A Day for the Dead by Uzo Emeruwa	25
The Long War by Callum Dunbar	26
World War One by Thaamaran Kuges	28
I have a Dream, by Robin Concepcion	29
Remembrance Day, by Aqeel Kashmiri	30
Polluted Seas by Thaamaran Kuges	31
Only If by Josiah Mbeledogu	32
A Perfect World by Lewis Chaffey	33
Imagine A World by Ahmed Mohamoud	34
If the World was Perfect by Kyran Scott	35
Perfect World for Me by Niraj Kuganathan	36
A Place where Everyone Could be Happy by Abdullah Zahid	37
A Perfect World by Zibyan Mohammed	38
Truth by Jamie Arrowsmith	39
Imagine a world by Ahmed Mohamoud	40
A Perfect World by Yahya Farhat	41

A Perfect World of Waffles by Kayden Abiri   43

Through the Eyes of a Soldier by Krushan Prakash   44

Dreams by Nayan Patel   46

The Captivity of Negativity by Zakareyah Hussain   48

Not by Ilyas Corneh   49

Copyright

All rights reserved.

The characters and events portrayed in this book are fictious. Any similarity to real persons, living or dead is coincidental and not intended by the author(s).

No part of this book may be reproduced, or stored in a retrieval system, or transmitted in any form or by any means, electronic, mechanical, photocopying, recording, or otherwise, without express written permission of the author.

ISBN: 9798340022370

Inspirational Quotes

"One learns from books and example only that certain things can be done. Actual learning requires that you do those things." — **Frank Herbert**

"Tell me and I forget, teach me and I may remember, involve me and I learn." — **Benjamin Franklin**

"True teachers are those who use themselves as bridges over which they invite their students to cross; then, having facilitated their crossing, joyfully collapse, encouraging them to create their own." — **Nikos Kazantzakis**

Introduction

Paulo Coelho De Souza (lyricist and novelist) once said that "People never learn anything by being told, they have to find out for themselves." At Ernest Bevin Academy, it is the goal of the English Department to create a love of learning English language and literature and celebrating this love of learning to master the art of poetry and creative writing. At Ernest Bevin Academy, students learn about themselves and the world through self-expression in the form of poetry.

From the moment students enter Ernest Bevin Academy, our English teachers set to work at dispelling and dismantling all the damaging preconceptions that tragically so many students pick up when they first look at a daunting poem. Our students spend a half term studying poetry every year, and what is more…they courageously try their hands at forming what at first seems so difficult. Here is a collection of that toil and endeavour. It is something that will be held for them for the rest of their lives…we hope it might enrich yours.

This book is the third anthology of poems written

by students at Ernest Bevin Academy. We are proud of our students and the hard work that they do and to celebrate their success we share their poems with you. This book is a compilation of the winners from the whole school creative writing Phoenix Competition and a combination of the works of students from the weekly running Poetry Club and creative writing workshops run by the English Department. It is through their poetry that they share their voice and from their voice that they are empowered to make a stand and speak out for all that they believe in.

They have considered the many challenges that we can face and like our school motto and logo, no matter what happens, we will rise like the phoenix.

We hope that you will enjoy reading these poems too as much as the staff and wider community of family and friends of Ernest Bevin Academy do.

A huge well done and many congratulations to the students at Ernest Bevin Academy.

I Wonder by Inam Ali

I wonder, I wonder, I wonder how it feels to live in a perfect world.
The world where I live is
Filled with terror, bullying, racism, slavery, poverty, no opportunity, no peace and no justice,
Millions of people die every day from hunger
No matter what we do, there will always be villains.
The world I wish for, the world I want, the world that I long for is:
A world filled with supreme wonders, with everything you need;
A place where everyone can live in peace and harmony,
A place where there is no poverty or hunger,
A place where all people can reach their full potential.
I wonder when the world will blossom like a cherry blossom.
I wonder, I wonder, I wonder …

A Perfect World by Niraj Kuganathan

Everyone wishes for some sort of perfect world
Where nobody gets bullied,
Where everyone can live forever,
Where everyone is rich,
And where little kids don't go hungry.
However, all this seems impossible.
We as humans need to work together to achieve such a thing
If it exists,
But we can't achieve it if we continue harm our planet,
What we call our home is being destroyed,
And it is turning into a crimson red abyss
Not able to keep safe, anyone.
We need to stop draining the oceans,
And polluting the air,
And cutting down trees.
We are the only ones that can stop this,
And create a perfect world.
We need to work together to achieve a perfect world,
And as the saying goes:

A COLLECTION OF CHILDREN'S POEMS

"Whatever you believe, you can achieve!"

Each Other by Connor Langley

Our world is ending,
Our minds are bending,
Our problems are never ending.
At the end of the day who can we trust,
The blood thirsty one we will never trust,
If we just collaborate with each other,
We could live with each other.

Despite our differences we are one,
In our minds number we are all number one,
But this gets in our way
And there is another way,
If we just worked each other,
We could live with each other.

We must work with each other,
So that we can live with each other.
We need one another,
We need each other.

A Perfect World
by Zaheer Gani

Peace not War,
War is gruesome.
Peace is happiness,
Peace is the key to life.

War is not the key to life,
War is people dying,
Peace is people living their best life.
War is nasty and gloomy.

Peace is the best thing we can have,
War is the worst thing we can have.
Take my advice and stop these wars,
Millions of people have died and are dying.

Let's create a perfect world.

Peace Not War by Abdullah Hoque

All I want is a perfect world where there is no war.
All I want is the world to be perfect from the core.
Everyone should be free.
Everyone should be happy.
Everyone would live a good life and feel loved
Everyone should sleep peacefully in their bed.
I want peace,
Not war.

A Perfect World by Robin Concepcion

There's a place that is perfect, I am sure.
There's a place where skies are sapphire seas,
And every breeze sings a melody of tranquillity.
There's a place like that.

Forests, with trees that touch the shining stars,
Whispering heavenly tunes to their verdant, lush leaves.
Deep within the heart of nature,
Flowers bloom and blossom in colours galore,
In this perfect heavenly world.

Cities and their districts are radiant with benevolence,
Streets as vast as rivers, awoken by laughter and joy,
Skyscrapers piercing into the starry sky.
There's a place like that,
I'm sure of it – a place that is perfect,
A perfect world.

A Perfect World by Malick Dieng Diallo

My perfect world is a place where there is freedom, and where I can fly with the birds high in the sky.

My perfect world is a place where people see our talents and not the way we look.

My perfect world is a place that black and white people act like brothers and sisters no matter how different they are

My perfect world is a place where there is no suffering and disease.

My perfect world is a place where there is no evil.

My perfect world is a place where there is no totalitarian and democracy everywhere.

My perfect world where there is no poverty.

My perfect world is where we do not need money to eat, where all have a home and there is equality.

A Perfect World by Oskar Maciag

A perfect world is:
A place where everyone is free,
And no dishonourable restrictions are in place,
Where no false convictions here held.

A perfect world is:
Where Mother Earth is clean,
Where all crimes are seen,
And people don't use gasoline.

A perfect world is:
Where there is no racial discrimination,
Where there is no need for frustration,
A place all people can get an education.

A perfect world is:
Where everyone is fed,
Where people achieve success,
And people are grateful for what they get.

A perfect world is:
Something so close, within our grasp,
And yet it is something so far.

A Perfect World by Ryad Muir

A perfect world is what we need,
To help all the people that are in need,
Poverty and starvation,
Has no place in our nation,
Wars and battles would not take place,
A perfect world is what we all want and need.

A Perfect World by Robin Concepcion

What is a perfect world if society cannot work together,
Where one side suffers, and the other one enjoys,
Where one side has everything, and the other one does not?
Many people endure hunger and poverty,
But there are some that have it all and do not appreciate what they have,
They waste on what they do not need,
And do not spend on what they really need.
The world needs healers not killers.
The world needs to be where people care for each other,
Like brothers and sisters.
The world should be a place where people share and do not take,
Where people forgive each other and move on.
We need a world where kindness spreads and hate compresses,
We need a world where there is peace and love, harmony, and hope.

It is not too late to make changes.
Hope is still around us and we need to come together with this hope to make a perfect world;
The perfect world where society is together, as one united -
A perfect world.

Through the Eyes of the Earth by Rory Langan

Every time a bullet goes off, I wince.
Every time humans cry, I do too.
But eventually my sympathy will run out.
They destroy what I gave them.
The glorious gift of life,
And not just the others,
But their own too.
What species is so stupid,
That they would dig their own grave and leap in?
The humans -
The species that I created, that's who!
Slowly I burn,
And it hurts
So very much.
Unbearable pain consumes me.
The species that I created,
Destroying me,
And there is nothing I can do but watch;
Watch as we all die together.

But I will survive,
I will live long after my creation perishes,
And I will recover.
My oceans are clean again,
And the trees are back once more.
The old human weapons are dead,
They are nothing but dust,
Such power no longer accessible,
And the loop begins again.
Another species rises,
And my destiny is sealed.
They will make me burn,
But I smile,
Because there is beauty in the chaos.
Such beauty.

Through their Eyes is Beauty by Jon-Lewis Odhiambo

Through their eyes I see the world anew,
A perspective so unique, so true.
Their gaze reveals a depth unknown,
Through their eyes I see the pain
The struggles they face, the loss, the strain,
But also, the beauty, the hope, the light -
A vision that shines ever so bright.
Through their eyes I see the truth,
The raw emotions, the forever trying youth.
Their clarity and vision are crystal clear,
They fight for what's right without fear.
Through their eyes I see the world in a different light,
A kaleidoscope of colours and emotions,
A tapestry woven with the treads of stories,
Through their eyes I see resilience and strength,
The vulnerability and the courage,
The endless possibilities of the human spirit.
Through their eyes I am reminded of the power of

empathy,
The importance of understanding,
The beauty of seeing the world through the eyes of another -
One I admire.

A Perfect World
by Sedad Assen

We dream of a perfect world,
A perfect world with no diseases,
A perfect world with no war,
A perfect world with no pain,
A perfect world with no death,
A perfect world with no suffering.
Yet we forget that perfection is not possible.
All we can do is try.

Freedom by Jack Broome

Freedom is a scarce thing across the global world
And it is divided into groups.
In this world freedom is for everyone
Freedom is what we need in this world today.

Freedom by Robin Concepcion

Deep in the heart of a forgotten world, where not even a ray of sunlight could pierce through, lies a sinner secured with the shackles of oppression.

The air is heavy, and the room where he resides is shrouded in darkness, the ground beneath breathes. In the distance, the unsettling sound of dripping water echoes ominously throughout the halls.

"Someone, help me!" pleads the sinner, desperately seeking for any presence of life amid the shadows.

Yet only silence speaks.

The sinner starts to navigate towards the hall of horrors before him, but every step felt like a descent into the abyss, and one step closer to death's cold embrace.

Amidst the darkness, the prisoner stood; his wrists and ankles were so tightly bounded by the shackles of his sins, it dug deep into his flesh.

Despite the darkness, he refused to succumb, however with each passing moment his hope waned.

Freedom by Malick Dieng Diallo

In a small town, there was a boy who wanted to be free.

Every day, he watched the birds fly in the sky and wished he could fly with them too.

The town had lots of strict rules, and he felt trapped.

One day, the boy saw a hole in the fence behind his house,

He decided to follow it, feeling happy to leave the rules behind.

He walked down the path, until he was finally free.

Freedom by Freddy Sheedy

Freedom!
A word many people did not understand
Until one man changed the way we see things;
A courageous man who fought for the equality of black people,
A man who wished to be accepted by white men for who he was,
And where he came from.
This brave man is Martin Luther King.
It all started in December 1955,
When Martin Luther King had had enough of racism,
He wanted a better life for all the black people.
In August of 1963, Luther gave his speech:
I have a dream.
This heartfelt speech won the hearts of hundreds of millions of people,
And with their support in America steps towards equality were taken.
Martin Luther King will always be remembered
In the hearts of many millions

As the founder of equality.
Freedom for all!
Freedom.

Love is in the Air by Jibril Abdul Wahab

Love is in the air,
Couples everywhere.
Love is beautiful;
It comes to us and fulfils.

Love is in the air,
Hours upon hours of love we share.
Love is our life,
For love we strive.

Love is valuable for us all,
And makes us happy for the rest of our lives.

An Unreachable World by Asvinth Sooriyapalan

In a world that just exists
With cities where water is scarce
Societies suffering - the list is endless
No one is left – all that is left is a bitter taste.
Nature is lost.
Where can people see the green grass and blue skies?
Where can people listen to rain and see green trees?
And here we are burdened by war.

A Day for the Dead by Uzo Emeruwa

We must close our eyes,
Look deep inside,
Look deep into our lives,
To see this beautiful life,
To appreciate what they did for us.
We feel as one, because they won
The war for us.
We give our gratitude,
For their patriotic attitude.
If these soldiers did not fight so bravely,
There would be no beautiful life
For you and me.
We give thanks to these men,
Who saved the lives of many.
We must always remember them
And what they did,
And have a day for the dead.

The Long War by Callum Dunbar

When the colonel shouts "go over the top"
I pray to God to make this stop, stop, stop!
The guns blast and boom,
And all I can see in the dark, dark gloom is
Fearful, nervous, and I am terrified -
I have nowhere to run or hide,
I look into the eyes of my friend,
And wonder how many of us will die.
This war has gone on forever,
It will never end,
All the men and all the horses,
Will they ever mend?

When the colonel shouts,
I fall on my knees,
And I pray to God, please, please, please!
I crawl in the mud,
And smell my friend's blood,
I see vision – my family and friends crying
As people are reported as dying.
I dream of going home safely one day,
As bullets fly by my ears,

In my head there are many fears.
This war has gone on forever,
It will never end.
All the men and all the horses,
Will they ever mend?

World War One by Thaamaran Kuges

In the trenches deep where the soldiers lay
They fought with valour day by day
The thunders of guns, the cries of pain
A war that brought so much disdain
From Flanders Fields to Somme – many died
They marched with courage, side by side
Brave hearts that beat with hope and fear
Their stories etched in history are clear
Through the mud and blood, they stood tall
Answering the call, they risked it all
For peace and unity together
We must remember these honourable soldiers forever.

I have a Dream, by Robin Concepcion

I have a dream,
That we will all live together as one.
I have a dream,
That inequality, injustice, discrimination will end,
That there will be a world, a utopia overflowing with love and peace
Where all can thrive and prosper.
I have a dream,
Where we all can laugh and live in harmony,
But here we are, confined by the manacles of prejudice.

Remembrance Day, by Aqeel Kashmiri

In trenches deep where brave hearts stood
Amongst the chaos the world withstood.
Nations clashed tired guns roared
As the soldier fought bravely their spirits roared.
The poppies bloomed an unforgettable symbol of lives lost
So, let's remember those who for us fought.
Let's never forget the courage of those men
We are here today because of them.

Polluted Seas by Thaamaran Kuges

Fish, dolphins, turtles
And more suffocating -
Dying because of us.
Plastic shoved in the waters.
We can stop this
If we come together
As one.
By recycling.
Putting rubbish
In the bin. This could save
The fish, dolphins, turtles
And more from dying.
We must stop pollution forever,
But only if we come together!

Only If by Josiah Mbeledogu

Sometimes we say, "only if …"
Only if we choose peace not war,
Only if the world was just pure,
Only if the world was rich and not poor.
In reality, there are only some things we can wish for …
Only if friendships remain intact and never break,
Only if we give and take,
Only if everyone observes the law,
In reality, there are only somethings that we can wish for ;
That inequality, prejudice, discrimination to go away -
One day …
If only. Only if.

A Perfect World by Lewis Chaffey

In a perfect world,
There would be no war,
There would be no hate,
There would be no greed,
And everyone would have food on their plates.

In a perfect world,
Everyone would be happy,
Everyone would be kind,
Everyone would be proud,
And everyone would achieve their dreams.

In our imperfect world,
Not everyone is happy,
Not everyone is kind,
Not everyone is proud,
Not everyone is at peace,
Not everyone has food on their plates,
And not everyone will achieve their dreams.

Imagine A World by Ahmed Mohamoud

Imagine a world with no hunger and no greed,
Imagine a world with no conflict just peace.
Kindness and friendship make this world great
But with conflict and war there are lives at stake.

Deforestation damages our Earth,
There are people around the world dying of thirst,
Being kind will put a smile on their face,
So, let's makes this world a perfect place.

We should leave negativity in the past,
To make our planet picture perfect at last.
Imagine a world with no hunger and no greed,
Imagine a world without conflict, and just peace.

If the World was Perfect by Kyran Scott

If the world was perfect, there would be no one in need.
We'd have clear skies, clean air, a warm sun and more trees.
If the world was perfect, we'd have no refugees.
We'd have no wars, just kindness and peace.
For a perfect world we need kindness, unity and clean seas.
If the whole world gave a helping hand,
There would be food on the table for every woman and man.
With a perfect world everyone would see
How great life could be.

Perfect World for Me by Niraj Kuganathan

A perfect world for me is where children can play video games with no restrictions,
Where people are nice and without frictions.
A perfect world is where oceans are clean, and the air is not polluted,
A perfect world is where nobody goes hungry,
A perfect world is where the grass is green on both sides,
A perfect world is where no one stresses,
A perfect world is where humans and animals live in harmony,
A perfect world is like the phoenix – it dies and is reborn stronger than before.
A perfect world can happen only if we act.

A Place where Everyone Could be Happy by Abdullah Zahid

A perfect world should be a place you want to be,
A perfect world should be a place you live free -
Where world hunger is a thing of the past,
Where homeless people won't be left for loss,
Where trees won't be cut down for people's greed …
We should always make space for a new seed.
War is such a cruel, cruel thing,
Why on people do we bring,
This devastation?
Why is the world littered with rubbish?
With greenhouse gasses on the rise,
That the world is falling apart is no surprise.
It is time to make a change,
So, let's make a place where we can all be happy,
A perfect world.

A Perfect World by Zibyan Mohammed

In a world where skies are always blue,
And every dream is bound to come true,
Children laugh and dance all day,
In this perfect world is where we all stay.

No tears are shed, no hearts are broken,
Every word is kind, every thoughtful act spoken.
Forests green and oceans clear,
Harmony reigns, and there is nothing to fear.

Truth by Jamie Arrowsmith

If you do not tell the truth about yourself,
You cannot tell it about other people.

Imagine a world by Ahmed Mohamoud

Imagine a world with no hunger, no greed,
Imagine a world with no conflict, just peace.
Kindness and friendship make this world great,
With conflict and war, our lives at stake.

Deforestation damages our earth,
People around the world dying of thirst,
Being kind will put smiles on faces,
So, let's make a world a perfect place.

We should leave negativity in the past,
To make our planet perfect at last,
Imagine a world with no hunger, no greed,
Imagine a world with no conflict, just peace.

A Perfect World by Yahya Farhat

A perfect world,
Lush greenery,
Amazing scenery.
A perfect world,
Glowing nights,
No more fights.
A perfect world,
No more wars,
Or unjust laws.
A perfect world,
No more plastic shores,
Not even any flaws.
Open your eyes,
It's just a dream,
It's not what it seems,
Open your eyes,
Look at the lies,
It's not what it seems.
Look at Gaza,
Look at the war,

Look at the poor.
Look at Gaza,
Look at the fights,
Look at the bombing in the night.
Look at humanity,
When goodness dies,
Evil will rise,
Say your goodbyes.

What is a perfect world?

A Perfect World of Waffles by Kayden Abiri

Waffles, waffles, waffles,
They rustle in the pocket,
Squish in your mouth,
As long as they don't expire,
They are all my desire,
Some shape like a fire,
Thumb shape in his square,
It does not matter,
Because I like them all,
Whether they are big or small.
If you run out of waffles,
The situation is most dire,
Because waffles are all that I desire,
They are perfect,
No matter the topping,
I love the heavenly taste and smell,
It will make your brain ring like a bell.

Through the Eyes of a Soldier by Krushan Prakash

We fight for them and their lives,
Here we are suffering with knives
In front of us are the safety camps,
Behind us all are the bombs guns and broken lamps,
Tiredness and exhaustion caught up with them and empty souls started sleeping,
Some of them were limping and some of them were bleeding;
They didn't even drink, yet they looked like drunks,
And they all started smelling badly like skunks.

They shouted out: Gas! Gas!
Danger occurred in a mass.
One man couldn't put his mask on and yelled out a lot,
This was the end for him as he started to rot.
His silhouette suffered poisonous smoke,
The soldier let out a deathly croak.

I can still see the soldier - I can envision him,

The picture I see is very dim.
The soldiers experienced the worst pain,
They always got left out in the cold stormy rain.
It is a struggle to see a man's death,
it is very hard to see him taking his last breath.
How would you feel if you saw man starting to decay?
How would you feel watching him rot away?
How would you feel if you heard a man scream?
This man, this soldier, dying like a shot bird?
For soldiers, the army is a sacrifice,
The number of deaths should not be a surprise.
We must respect the soldiers that die,
Because they did more than try.

Dreams by Nayan Patel

What's the point of dreams if you leave them on your pillow,
Your aspirations are what makes you, you.
The picture that you make is the picture that you paint,
So don't let anyone tell you what you can and cannot do.
Imagine you are 33, and you don't want to be,
Because you gave up on your silly little dream ...
It's your future at stake; the life you wanted,
Happiness is the main measure of your success,
Don't give up on your dreams that you want to have,
Regret is way worse than rejection,
So, don't let anyone tell you what you can and cannot do,
Because being yourself is being true to you.
Say hello to your dreams and ignore the voices
Telling you this and that,
When you could be this or that.
Pick up your paint brush and explore your world -
Who you want to become is up to you -

Now you've made your picture – get to your painting
Your dreams.

The Captivity of Negativity by Zakareyah Hussain

When life has you down on the low
With nowhere inspirational to go,
It is important to always remember to reach high,
Stretching high up to the sky.
You may need help along the way,
And that is what friends are for ...
To make sure from positivity you don't sway
And to help open the doors -
To escape the captivity of negativity.

Not by Ilyas Corneh

When they ask me how I'm feeling
I say, I'm fine, but I'm not.
When they say I should smile,
I say, sure, but I won't.
When they ask about Palestine,
I say, I hope they'll be fine, but they're not.
When they ask me to be kind
I say, I'll try, but I won't.
If they ask about my homework
I say, I forgot, but I did not.
When they ask about people who have died,
I say, it happens, but it should not.
Sometimes, I wish I could just tell the truth,
But I don't.